Great Works

Instruction for Literature

My Brother Sam Is Dead

A guide for the novel by James Lincoln Collier and Christopher Collier
Great Works Author: Suzanne Barchers

SHELL EDUCATION

Image Credits

Gettyimages, Superstock, Brown & Bigelow, St. Paul and Toronto, Reproduction of 1907 painting by John Ward Dunsmore (cover)

Standards

© 2007 Teachers of English to Speakers of Other Languages, Inc. (TESOL)
© 2007 Board of Regents of the University of Wisconsin System. World-Class Instructional Design and Assessment (WIDA)
© Copyright 2010 National Governors Association Center for Best Practices and Council of Chief State School Officers. All rights reserved

Shell Education
5301 Oceanus Drive
Huntington Beach, CA 92649-1030
http://www.shelleducation.com
ISBN 978-1-4258-8984-5
© 2014 Shell Educational Publishing, Inc.

Table of Contents

How to Use This Literature Guide

Today's standards demand rigor and relevance in the reading of complex texts. The units in this series guide teachers in a rich and deep exploration of worthwhile works of literature for classroom study. The most rigorous instruction can also be interesting and engaging!

Many current strategies for effective literacy instruction have been incorporated into these instructional guides for literature. Throughout the units, text-dependent questions are used to determine comprehension of the book as well as student interpretation of the vocabulary words. The books chosen for the series are complex exemplars of carefully crafted works of literature. Close reading is used throughout the units to guide students toward revisiting the text and using textual evidence to respond to prompts orally and in writing. Students must analyze the story elements in multiple assignments for each section of the book. All of these strategies work together to rigorously guide students through their study of literature.

The next few pages will make clear how to use this guide for a purposeful and meaningful literature study. Each section of this guide is set up in the same way to make it easier for you to implement the instruction in your classroom.

Theme Thoughts

The great works of literature used throughout this series have important themes that have been relevant to people for many years. Many of the themes will be discussed during the various sections of this instructional guide. However, it would also benefit students to have independent time to think about the key themes of the novel.

Before students begin reading, have them complete *Pre-Reading Theme Thoughts* (page 13). This graphic organizer will allow students to think about the themes outside the context of the story. They'll have the opportunity to evaluate statements based on important themes and defend their opinions. Be sure to have students keep their papers for comparison to the *Post-Reading Theme Thoughts* (page 64). This graphic organizer is similar to the pre-reading activity. However, this time, students will be answering the questions from the point of view of one of the characters of the novel. They have to think about how the character would feel about each statement and defend their thoughts. To conclude the activity, have students compare what they thought about the themes before they read the novel to what the characters discovered during the story.

How to Use This Literature Guide *(cont.)*

Vocabulary

Each teacher overview page has definitions and sentences about how key vocabulary words are used in the section. These words should be introduced and discussed with students. There are two student vocabulary activity pages in each section. On the first page, students are asked to define the ten words chosen by the author of this unit. On the second page in most sections, each student will select at least eight words that he or she finds interesting or difficult. For each section, choose one of these pages for your students to complete. With either assignment, you may want to have students get into pairs to discuss the meanings of the words. Allow students to use reference guides to define the words. Monitor students to make sure the definitions they have found are accurate and relate to how the words are used in the text.

On some of the vocabulary student pages, students are asked to answer text-related questions about the vocabulary words. The following question stems will help you create your own vocabulary questions if you'd like to extend the discussion.

- How does this word describe _____'s character?
- In what ways does this word relate to the problem in this story?
- How does this word help you understand the setting?
- In what ways is this word related to the story's solution?
- Describe how this word supports the novel's theme of . . . .
- What visual images does this word bring to your mind?
- For what reasons might the author have chosen to use this particular word?

At times, more work with the words will help students understand their meanings. The following quick vocabulary activities are a good way to further study the words.

- Have students practice their vocabulary and writing skills by creating sentences and/or paragraphs in which multiple vocabulary words are used correctly and with evidence of understanding.

- Students can play vocabulary concentration. Students make a set of cards with the words and a separate set of cards with the definitions. Then, students lay the cards out on the table and play concentration. The goal of the game is to match vocabulary words with their definitions.

- Students can create word journal entries about the words. Students choose words they think are important and then describe why they think each word is important within the novel.

How to Use This Literature Guide *(cont.)*

Analyzing the Literature

After students have read each section, hold small-group or whole-class discussions. Questions are written at two levels of complexity to allow you to decide which questions best meet the needs of your students. The Level 1 questions are typically less abstract than the Level 2 questions. Level 1 is indicated by a square, while Level 2 is indicated by a triangle. These questions focus on the various story elements, such as character, setting, and plot. Student pages are provided if you want to assign these questions for individual student work before your group discussion. Be sure to add further questions as your students discuss what they've read. For each question, a few key points are provided for your reference as you discuss the novel with students.

Reader Response

In today's classrooms, there are often great readers who are below average writers. So much time and energy is spent in classrooms getting students to read on grade level, that little time is left to focus on writing skills. To help teachers include more writing in their daily literacy instruction, each section of this guide has a literature-based reader response prompt. Each of the three genres of writing is used in the reader responses within this guide: narrative, informative/explanatory, and argument. Students have a choice between two prompts for each reader response. One response requires students to make connections between the reading and their own lives. The other prompt requires students to determine text-to-text connections or connections within the text.

Close Reading the Literature

Within each section, students are asked to closely reread a short section of text. Since some versions of the novels have different page numbers, the selections are described by chapter and location, along with quotations to guide the readers. After each close reading, there are text-dependent questions to be answered by students.

Encourage students to read each question one at a time and then go back to the text and discover the answer. Work with students to ensure that they use the text to determine their answers rather than making unsupported inferences. Once students have answered the questions, discuss what they discovered. Suggested answers are provided in the answer key.

How to Use This Literature Guide *(cont.)*

Close Reading the Literature *(cont.)*

The generic, open-ended stems below can be used to write your own text-dependent questions if you would like to give students more practice.

- Give evidence from the text to support . . . .
- Justify your thinking using text evidence about . . . .
- Find evidence to support your conclusions about . . . .
- What text evidence helps the reader understand . . . ?
- Use the book to tell why _____ happens.
- Based on events in the story, ...
- Use text evidence to describe why . . . .

Making Connections

The activities in this section help students make cross-curricular connections to writing, mathematics, science, social studies, or the fine arts. Each of these types of activities requires higher-order thinking skills from students.

Creating with the Story Elements

It is important to spend time discussing the common story elements in literature. Understanding the characters, setting, and plot can increase students' comprehension and appreciation of the story. If teachers discuss these elements daily, students will more likely internalize the concepts and look for the elements in their independent reading. Another important reason for focusing on the story elements is that students will be better writers if they think about how the stories they read are constructed.

Students are given three options for working with the story elements. They are asked to create something related to the characters, setting, or plot of the novel. Students are given a choice on this activity so that they can decide to complete the activity that most appeals to them. Different multiple intelligences are used so that the activities are diverse and interesting to all students.

How to Use This Literature Guide (cont.)

Culminating Activity

This open-ended, cross-curricular activity requires higher-order thinking and allows for a creative product. Students will enjoy getting the chance to share what they have discovered through reading the novel. Be sure to allow them enough time to complete the activity at school or home.

Comprehension Assessment

The questions in this section are modeled after current standardized tests to help students analyze what they've read and prepare for tests they may see in their classrooms. The questions are dependent on the text and require critical-thinking skills to answer.

Response to Literature

The final post-reading activity is an essay based on the text that also requires further research by students. This is a great way to extend this book into other curricular areas. A suggested rubric is provided for teacher reference.

Correlation to the Standards

Shell Education is committed to producing educational materials that are research and standards based. As part of this effort, we have correlated all of our products to the academic standards of all 50 states, the District of Columbia, the Department of Defense Dependents Schools, and all Canadian provinces.

Purpose and Intent of Standards

Standards are designed to focus instruction and guide adoption of curricula. Standards are statements that describe the criteria necessary for students to meet specific academic goals. They define the knowledge, skills, and content students should acquire at each level. Standards are also used to develop standardized tests to evaluate students' academic progress. Teachers are required to demonstrate how their lessons meet standards. Standards are used in the development of all of our products, so educators can be assured they meet high academic standards.

How to Find Standards Correlations

To print a customized correlation report of this product for your state, visit our website at http://www.shelleducation.com and follow the online directions. If you require assistance in printing correlation reports, please contact our Customer Service Department at 1-877-777-3450.

Correlation to the Standards (cont.)

Standards Correlation Chart

The lessons in this guide were written to support the Common Core College and Career Readiness Anchor Standards. This chart indicates which sections of this guide address the anchor standards.

Common Core College and Career Readiness Anchor Standard	Section
CCSS.ELA-Literacy.CCRA.R.1—Read closely to determine what the text says explicitly and to make logical inferences from it; cite specific textual evidence when writing or speaking to support conclusions drawn from the text.	Close Reading the Literature Sections 1–5; Making Connections Sections 1–3; Creating with the Story Elements Sections 1, 3–5; Culminating Activity
CCSS.ELA-Literacy.CCRA.R.2—Determine central ideas or themes of a text and analyze their development; summarize the key supporting details and ideas.	Analyzing the Literature Sections 1–5; Making Connections Sections 1–2, 5; Pre-Reading Theme Thoughts
CCSS.ELA-Literacy.CCRA.R.3—Analyze how and why individuals, events, or ideas develop and interact over the course of a text.	Analyzing the Literature Sections 1–5; Creating with the Story Elements Sections 1–5; Making Connections Sections 1, 3
CCSS.ELA-Literacy.CCRA.R.4—Interpret words and phrases as they are used in a text, including determining technical, connotative, and figurative meanings, and analyze how specific word choices shape meaning or tone.	Vocabulary Sections 1–5
CCSS.ELA-Literacy.CCRA.R.5—Analyze the structure of texts, including how specific sentences, paragraphs, and larger portions of the text (e.g., a section, chapter, scene, or stanza) relate to each other and the whole.	Making Connections Section 2; Creating with the Story Elements Sections 1–5; Culminating Activity
CCSS.ELA-Literacy.CCRA.W.1—Write arguments to support claims in an analysis of substantive topics or texts using valid reasoning and relevant and sufficient evidence.	Reader Response Sections 2, 4; Post-Reading Response to Literature
CCSS.ELA-Literacy.CCRA.W.2—Write informative/explanatory texts to examine and convey complex ideas and information clearly and accurately through the effective selection, organization, and analysis of content.	Reader Response Sections 1–5; Culminating Activity; Post-Reading Response to Literature
CCSS.ELA-Literacy.CCRA.W.3—Write narratives to develop real or imagined experiences or events using effective technique, well-chosen details and well-structured event sequences.	Reader Response Sections 1, 3, 5; Creating with the Story Elements Sections 2, 4; Culminating Activity; Post-Reading Response to Literature

Correlation to the Standards (cont.)

Standards Correlation Chart (cont.)

Common Core College and Career Readiness Anchor Standard	Section
CCSS.ELA-Literacy.CCRA.W.4—Produce clear and coherent writing in which the development, organization, and style are appropriate to task, purpose, and audience.	Creating with the Story Elements Sections 2, 4; Reader Response Sections 1–5; Culminating Activity; Post-Reading Response to Literature
CCSS.ELA-Literacy.CCRA.W.6—Use technology, including the Internet, to produce and publish writing and to interact and collaborate with others.	Post-Reading Response to Literature
CCSS.ELA-Literacy.CCRA.W.9—Draw evidence from literary or informational texts to support analysis, reflection, and research.	Making Connections Sections 1–2, 4; Creating with the Story Elements Section 5; Post-Reading Response to Literature
CCSS.ELA-Literacy.CCRA.L.1—Demonstrate command of the conventions of standard English grammar and usage when writing or speaking.	Creating with the Story Elements Sections 2, 4; Reader Response Sections 1–5; Culminating Activity; Post-Reading Response to Literature
CCSS.ELA-Literacy.CCRA.L.4—Determine or clarify the meaning of unknown and multiple-meaning words and phrases by using context clues, analyzing meaningful word parts, and consulting general and specialized reference materials, as appropriate.	Vocabulary Sections 1–5
CCSS.ELA-Literacy.CCRA.L.6—Acquire and use accurately a range of general academic and domain-specific words and phrases sufficient for reading, writing, speaking, and listening at the college and career readiness level; demonstrate independence in gathering vocabulary knowledge when encountering an unknown term important to comprehension or expression.	Vocabulary Sections 1–5

TESOL and WIDA Standards

The lessons in this book promote English language development for English language learners. The following TESOL and WIDA English Language Development Standards are addressed through the activities in this book:

- **Standard 1:** English language learners communicate for social and instructional purposes within the school setting.
- **Standard 2:** English language learners communicate information, ideas and concepts necessary for academic success in the content area of language arts.

About the Authors—James Lincoln Collier and Christopher Collier

James Lincoln Collier was born into a family of writers on June 27, 1928. His brother, Christopher, was born a year and a half later on January 29, 1930. James built a writing and editing career and also played trombone professionally. Christopher, also a musician, completed a doctorate degree in history. He taught history to junior high through college level students.

Christopher focused on scholarly writing for years, with one book receiving a Pulitzer Prize nomination. James, who wrote for children and young adults, routinely "hounded" Christopher to help him write historical novels for young readers. Their collaboration on *My Brother Sam Is Dead* led to a Newbery Honor Award, a Notable Book designation by the American Library Association, and a nomination for a National Book Award in 1975. The book also received the Phoenix Honor Award in honor of its longevity and excellence in 1994.

The brothers have fine-tuned their collaborative process over the years. After determining the historical event for the book's focus, Christopher begins his research. From the weather, to the terrain, to the customs of the time, he gathers information that will ensure authenticity. He sends his research and an outline of the book to James, who then begins writing the first draft. James builds on Christopher's work, saying that he might take the book in whatever direction he wishes, but that he uses the foundation of that early research. The brothers continue researching the details while passing drafts back and forth, sometimes visiting a particular site to verify the information.

The Colliers continue to collaborate on a variety of novels on topics they consider of high importance to young people. They are not afraid to tackle tough issues, such as those found in *My Brother Sam Is Dead*. Their Arabus Family Saga series, with its treatment of slavery, is as highly regarded as their other books about war.

Possible Texts for Text Comparisons

The Bloody Country explores the effects of the Revolutionary War on mill owners and their slaves. *The Winter Hero* is set in 1787 and explores Shays' Rebellion. As with *My Brother Sam Is Dead*, a family is embroiled in political and personal conflicts. The Arabus Family Saga series explores the role of African Americans during and after the Revolutionary War. This series includes *War Comes to Willy Freeman*, *Jump Ship to Freedom*, and *Who Is Carrie?*

Book Summary of *My Brother Sam Is Dead*

As with many families of the Revolutionary era, members of the Meeker family have different opinions about remaining loyal to Great Britain or not. Sam, who is attending college, comes home to Redding, Connecticut, and informs his family that he intends to fight with the Patriots. His father, who is a staunch Loyalist, forbids Sam to go. Sam steals his father's gun and joins the continental soldiers in their rebellion.

Tim, the young narrator of the story, admires his older brother, Sam. But he is also loyal to his father. As the war unfolds, the tasks involved in maintaining the family tavern become more arduous. Everyone works long and hard in Sam's absence, and the fracture in the family becomes permanent when Tim's father, Life, is arrested by the Patriots as a traitor. Life dies on a British prison ship—a bitter irony considering that he is loyal to the king—leaving Tim and his mother to run the family tavern alone.

During a brief, unauthorized visit home, Sam and Tim hear thieves stealing their cattle. Sam pursues the men, who turn out to be fellow soldiers. They turn on Sam, claiming that he is the thief. Sam is arrested for stealing his own cattle, and the commanding general decides to make an example of him. Despite Sam's family's best efforts to clear his name, Sam is executed.

Note: The Colliers' meticulous research into the period includes the use of language and practices of the time. This book has been challenged because it includes profanity, violence, and alcohol consumption. (In fact, the Meekers' inn is where alcohol is served.) After you preread the book, you may consider these options: proceed with the use of the book; read the book aloud, modifying the text as necessary; or have parents sign a waiver stating that they understand that this award-winning book uses profanity and describes events consistent with the Revolutionary War.

Cross-Curricular Connection

This book can be used for social studies during a study of the American Revolution or during a unit on war.

Possible Texts for Text Sets

- Brady, Esther Wood. *Toliver's Secret*. Yearling, 1993.
- Forbes, Esther. *Johnny Tremain*. HMH Books for Young Readers, 2011.
- McGovern, Ann. *The Secret Soldier: The Story of Deborah Sampson*. Scholastic Paperbacks, 1990.
- O'Dell, Scott. *Sarah Bishop*. HMH Books for Young Readers, 1980.

Name _____

Date _____

Pre-Reading Theme Thoughts

Directions: Read each of the statements in the first column. Decide if you agree or disagree with the statements. Record your opinion by marking an **X** in Agree or Disagree for each statement. Explain your choices in the fourth column. There are no right or wrong answers.

Statement	Agree	Disagree	Explain Your Answer
It's okay to steal food to survive.			
Families should stick together during tough times.			
A teenager can rebel if he or she thinks a parent is wrong.			
Killing during times of war is always justified.			

Vocabulary Overview

Ten key words from this section are provided below with definitions and sentences about how the words are used in the book. Choose one of the vocabulary activity sheets (pages 15 or 16) for students to complete as they read this section. Monitor students as they work to ensure the definitions they have found are accurate and relate to the text. Finally, discuss these important vocabulary words with students. If you think these words or other words in the section warrant more time devoted to them, there are suggestions in the introduction for other vocabulary activities (page 5).

Word	Definition	Sentence about Text
massacred (ch. 1)	killed; destroyed	The minutemen hide and **massacre** the British soldiers.
rebellion (ch. 1)	revolution; fighting back	Shooting at the British soldiers is an act of **rebellion**.
constitutes (ch. 1)	equals	Sam's father decides for himself what **constitutes** treason.
agitators (ch. 1)	activists	Those **agitators** want others to join the fight.
civil (ch. 1)	courteous; polite	Children should be **civil** and not rude.
inscription (ch. 1)	writing; message	The **inscription** in Sam's book is hard to read.
sloth (ch. 1)	laziness	Tim knows that work is better than **sloth**.
scornful (ch. 2)	disrespectful; disdainful	Sam's father is **scornful** when he talks about Sam's ideas.
subversion (ch. 3)	treason	Sam's father says that criticizing the king is **subversion**.
idling (ch. 3)	sitting around	Mother tells Betsy she should be busy, not **idling**.

Name _____

Date _____

Understanding Vocabulary Words

Directions: The following words appear in this section of the book. Use context clues and reference materials to determine an accurate definition for each word.

Word	Definition
massacred (ch. 1)	
rebellion (ch. 1)	
constitutes (ch. 1)	
agitators (ch. 1)	
civil (ch. 1)	
inscription (ch. 1)	
sloth (ch. 1)	
scornful (ch. 2)	
subversion (ch. 3)	
idling (ch. 3)	

Name _____

Date _____

During-Reading Vocabulary Activity

Directions: As you read these chapters, record at least eight important words on the lines below. Try to find interesting, difficult, intriguing, special, or funny words. Your words can be long or short. They can be hard or easy to spell. After each word, use context clues in the text and reference materials to define the word.

- _____
- _____
- _____
- _____
- _____
- _____
- _____
- _____
- _____

Directions: Respond to these questions about the words in this section.

1. How does Father feel about **treason**?

_____

_____

2. What can you conclude about Sam's **triumphs** from his time in college?

_____

_____

Analyzing the Literature

Provided below are discussion questions you can use in small groups, with the whole class, or for written assignments. Each question is given at two levels so you can choose the right question for each group of students. Activity sheets with these questions are provided (pages 18–19) if you want students to write their responses. For each question, a few key discussion points are provided for your reference.

Story Element	■ Level 1	▲ Level 2	Key Discussion Points
Plot	How does Sam's father react when Sam comes home in a uniform?	Contrast Tim's reaction to Sam's arrival in uniform with his father's reaction. How are the reactions alike and different?	Discuss how everyone is shocked to see Sam in a uniform. Explore how Father disagrees with Sam, arguing with him. Tim, in contrast, is happy to see Sam, and he's unsure about who is right—his father or Sam.
Setting	What kind of home and business do the Meekers have?	What kind of work does the family do to run the tavern and farm?	The Meekers own a tavern, living above it. Everyone in the family works: cooking and serving food, milking the cows, chopping wood, raising food, and so forth.
Plot	What does Sam do to upset the family when he leaves?	How does Tim react to Sam's theft?	Sam steals their father's musket, called Brown Bess. Tim finds out and insists they need it at home. He also realizes that Sam needs it as a soldier. He cries at first, but eventually he stops crying out of shame.
Character	Why does Betsy hang around the tavern so much?	Do you think Betsy should tell Tim when Sam is going to visit? Why or why not?	Discuss how Betsy and Sam might be sweet on each other. She is trying to ensure that Tim won't tell on Sam if he visits. Tim would be betraying his father by not telling. Yet, Tim misses Sam.

Name _____

Date _____

Analyzing the Literature

Directions: Think about the section you just read. Read each question and state your response with textual evidence.

1. How does Sam's father react when Sam comes home in a uniform?

_____

_____

_____

_____

2. What kind of home and business do the Meekers have?

_____

_____

_____

_____

3. What does Sam do to upset the family when he leaves?

_____

_____

_____

_____

4. Why does Betsy hang around the tavern so much?

_____

_____

_____

_____

Name _____

Date _____

▲ Analyzing the Literature

Directions: Think about the section you just read. Read each question and state your response with textual evidence.

1. Contrast Tim's reaction to Sam's arrival in uniform with his father's reaction. How are the reactions alike and different?

_____

_____

_____

_____

2. What kind of work does the family do to run the tavern and farm?

_____

_____

_____

_____

3. How does Tim react to Sam's theft?

_____

_____

_____

_____

4. Do you think Betsy should tell Tim when Sam is going to visit? Why or why not?

_____

_____

_____

Name _____

Date _____

Reader Response

Directions: Choose one of the following prompts about this section to answer. Be sure you include a topic sentence in your response, use textual evidence to support your opinion, and provide a strong conclusion that summarizes your opinion.

Writing Prompts

- **Narrative Piece**—Think about the tensions Tim faces because of Sam's departure. Write him a letter of encouragement and advice as if you were his best friend or close cousin. Draw upon your own experiences with handling difficult family situations.
- **Informative/Explanatory Piece**—Write two contrasting statements. One should be from Sam explaining why he is going to war. The other statement should be from his brother or his father, explaining his position.

_____

_____

_____

_____

_____

_____

_____

_____

_____

_____

_____

_____

_____

Close Reading the Literature

Directions: Closely reread the section toward the end of chapter 1 that starts with "Principle, Sam?" Read through the end of the chapter. Read each question, and then revisit the text to find the evidence that supports your answer.

1. Father describes war to Sam. Give two examples from the book of things he *heard* during his time at Louisbourg.

   _____

   _____

   _____

2. Find two examples in this section that tell what Father does *not* want for Sam.

   _____

   _____

   _____

3. How does Sam feel about the argument? Use words from this section of the story for your answer.

   _____

   _____

   _____

4. What event tells you that Tim knows there are bad times coming? Support your answer with evidence from the story.

   _____

   _____

   _____

Name _____

Date _____

Making Connections–Taking Sides

Sam's father has definite opinions about the right thing to do. How would an adult in your family react if you decided to fight against a king? Write Father's reactions to each event. Then, write how an adult in your family would react.

Event	Father's Reaction	Your Family's Reaction
Leaving college to fight against the government		
Arguing with parents in a public setting		
Stealing the family's only weapon		

Name _____

Date _____

Creating with the Story Elements

Directions: Thinking about the story elements of character, setting, and plot in a novel is very important to understanding what is happening and why. Complete **one** of the following activities about what you've read so far. Be creative and have fun!

Characters

Create a recruitment poster for the Patriots. List characteristics of good soldiers. For ideas, think about Sam and his ideals. You can also look at pictures of recruitment posters, flags from the 1700s, and other historical images.

Setting

Reread the section in chapter 1 that describes the tavern. Make a cutaway model of the tavern. A cutaway model has one wall removed so that the inside layout and details can be seen. It can be a drawing or a three-dimensional version.

Plot

There are several turning points in this section: Sam comes home from college in a uniform; Sam and Father argue; Sam tells Tim he's going to fight in Massachusetts; Sam steals the musket; Sam's father tells him to leave; Betsy tells Tim that Sam has written to her, and so on. Choose one turning point. Create a drawing or single-panel cartoon that shows that moment. Give it a caption that captures the main idea of that moment in the story.

Vocabulary Overview

Ten key words from this section are provided below with definitions and sentences about how the words are used in the book. Choose one of the vocabulary activity sheets (pages 25 or 26) for students to complete as they read this section. Monitor students as they work to ensure the definitions they have found are accurate and relate to the text. Finally, discuss these important vocabulary words with students. If you think these words or other words in the section warrant more time devoted to them, there are suggestions in the introduction for other vocabulary activities (page 5).

Word	Definition	Sentence about Text
traitors (ch. 4)	defectors; people acting against the government	Father is loyal to the king, but feels that other men are **traitors**.
clambering (ch. 4)	scrambling	Tim runs through the pastures, **clambering** over fences.
ramrod (ch. 4)	rod used to load a musket	Sam uses the **ramrod** and loads his musket quickly.
commissary (ch. 5)	supplies and food	The army **commissary** officers need food for the men.
petition (ch. 5)	written request	People sometimes sign a **petition** that lists their demands.
cipher (ch. 5)	do math	Tim is good with numbers and likes to **cipher**.
surveyor (ch. 5)	someone who studies land	Being a land **surveyor** would be a good job for Tim.
apprentice (ch. 5)	someone being trained	Tim could learn from another surveyor as an **apprentice**.
speculating (ch. 5)	investing in something with a risk of loss	**Speculating** on buying land might pay off.
cholera (ch. 5)	stomach illness that is like the flu	**Cholera** is a miserable disease that can lead to death.

Name _____

Date _____

Understanding Vocabulary Words

Directions: The following words appear in this section of the book. Use context clues and reference materials to determine an accurate definition for each word.

Word	Definition
traitors (ch. 4)	
clambering (ch. 4)	
ramrod (ch. 4)	
commissary (ch. 5)	
petition (ch. 5)	
cipher (ch. 5)	
surveyor (ch. 5)	
apprentice (ch. 5)	
speculating (ch. 5)	
cholera (ch. 5)	

Name _____

Date _____

During-Reading Vocabulary Activity

Directions: As you read these chapters, record at least eight important words on the lines below. Try to find interesting, difficult, intriguing, special, or funny words. Your words can be long or short. They can be hard or easy to spell. After each word, use context clues in the text and reference materials to define the word.

- _____
- _____
- _____
- _____
- _____
- _____
- _____
- _____
- _____

Directions: Respond to these questions about the words in this section.

1. Why would the Patriots be thought of as **underdogs** in their battles?

_____

_____

2. In chapter 6, why does Tim think that he is being **dishonorable**?

_____

_____

_____

Analyzing the Literature

Provided below are discussion questions you can use in small groups, with the whole class, or for written assignments. Each question is given at two levels so you can choose the right question for each group of students. Activity sheets with these questions are provided (pages 28–29) if you want students to write their responses. For each question, a few key discussion points are provided for your reference.

Story Element	■ Level 1	▲ Level 2	Key Discussion Points
Plot	What do the soldiers want from Tim's father in chapter 6? Why?	Why does Tim say that the war has come to Redding in chapter 6? Who is right, the Rebels or his father?	Discuss how the rebel soldiers are collecting weapons, necessary for their fight. For Tim, the conflict has become real because his father is hurt.
Character	Why doesn't Sam agree to return the musket?	Sam has sneaked home, so he refuses to return the musket. What does that tell you about Sam's character?	Discuss the notion of "everyone does it," Sam's excuse for sneaking home. Apply the concept to times when kids are tempted to break rules.
Setting	How does Tim work out a way to deliver the letter?	What is Tim's motivation for trying to deliver the letter?	Tim realizes he can pretend to go fishing. He wants to do something important in the war effort so he can tell Sam about it.
Plot	What event ruins Tim's journey with the letter?	How does Mr. Heron test Tim? Is he right not to trust Tim? Is Betsy right in what she did?	Betsy realizes that Sam is delivering a letter for Mr. Heron. She grabs and opens it. There is no right answer—both Mr. Heron and Betsy have some valid reasons for their actions, as does Tim.

Name _____

Date _____

Analyzing the Literature

Directions: Think about the section you just read. Read each question and state your response with textual evidence.

1. What do the soldiers want from Tim's father in chapter 6? Why?

    _____

    _____

    _____

    _____

2. Why doesn't Sam agree to return the musket?

    _____

    _____

    _____

    _____

3. How does Tim work out a way to deliver the letter?

    _____

    _____

    _____

    _____

4. What event ruins Tim's journey with the letter?

    _____

    _____

    _____

    _____

Name _____

Date _____

▲ Analyzing the Literature

Directions: Think about the section you just read. Read each question and state your response with textual evidence.

1. Why does Tim say that the war has come to Redding in chapter 6? Who is right, the Rebels or his father?

   _____

   _____

   _____

2. Sam has sneaked home, so he refuses to return the musket. What does that tell you about Sam's character?

   _____

   _____

   _____

3. What is Tim's motivation for trying to deliver the letter?

   _____

   _____

   _____

4. How does Mr. Heron test Tim? Is he right not to trust Tim? Is Betsy right in what she did?

   _____

   _____

   _____

   _____

Name _____

Date _____

Reader Response

Directions: Choose one of the following prompts about this section to answer. Be sure you include a topic sentence in your response, use textual evidence to support your opinion, and provide a strong conclusion that summarizes your opinion.

Writing Prompts

- **Opinion/Argument Piece**—There are two sides to every situation. Which side are you on, Betsy's or Mr. Heron's? Explain who you think is right.
- **Informative/Explanatory Piece**—As the war begins, everything feels like a story to Tim. In this section, Tim begins to think of the war as "real." Explain why his feelings have changed.

_____

_____

_____

_____

_____

_____

_____

_____

_____

_____

_____

_____

_____

_____

Name _____

Date _____

Close Reading the Literature

Directions: Closely reread the first four paragraphs of chapter 5. Read each question, then revisit the text to find the evidence that supports your answer.

1. Drawing from the first paragraph, give at least two examples of war stories.

   _____

   _____

   _____

   _____

2. Why does the war seem like a story to Tim at first? Give at least two reasons from the section.

   _____

   _____

   _____

   _____

3. For what reasons does the war seem real to Tim now?

   _____

   _____

   _____

   _____

4. Using the text for examples, explain the value of guns to the people in the area.

   _____

   _____

   _____

Name _____

Date _____

Making Connections–Putting Up Defenses

Directions: Think about the different ways people can defend themselves: weapons, words, physical force, deceit, a petition, fences, negotiation, and so forth. Read the events in the first column. Imagine that you are Tim's age, living on a farm next to his tavern. Describe how you would defend yourself during the war. Be thoughtful in explaining your choices.

Event	Your Response
Starving soldiers are stealing your cows.	
Soldiers are camping in your fields. It's time to plant crops.	
Your best friend is for one side in the war. You are for the other. Your friend says you're stupid for being for that side.	
An adult says it's a sin to fight in any war. Yet, your brother is fighting for what you both believe is right.	

Name _____

Date _____

Creating with the Story Elements

Directions: Thinking about the story elements of character, setting, and plot in a novel is very important to understanding what is happening and why. Complete **one** of the following activities about what you've read so far. Be creative and have fun!

Characters

Giving 360-degree feedback means looking at something from all sides. Do a 360-degree profile on Betsy. Write short descriptions of Betsy from the points of view of the following characters: Mr. Meeker, Mrs. Meeker, Tim, and Sam.

Setting

The Meekers live in farming country. The soldiers from both sides are butchering cows. Write a petition like the people might have written. It should describe how the presence of the soldiers affects the countryside, animals, and people's lives. Include your demands—what you want the soldiers to do or stop doing.

Plot

What might happen if Tim delivers the letter? Write an outline for a chapter that explains what happens. Be imaginative and think about all the things that could go right or wrong.

Vocabulary Overview

Ten key words from this section are provided below with definitions and sentences about how the words are used in the book. Choose one of the vocabulary activity sheets (pages 35 or 36) for students to complete as they read this section. Monitor students as they work to ensure the definitions they have found are accurate and relate to the text. Finally, discuss these important vocabulary words with students. If you think these words or other words in the section warrant more time devoted to them, there are suggestions in the introduction for other vocabulary activities (page 5).

Word	Definition	Sentence about Text
enlistment (ch. 7)	enrollment in the army	Soldiers go home when their **enlistment** is over.
recalcitrance (ch. 7)	stubbornness	Sam doesn't give in, showing his **recalcitrance**.
grimace (ch. 7)	scowl; show frustration	After the cow-boy pulls his gun, Father **grimaces** and shakes his head.
slaughter (ch. 8)	kill; destroy	During the war some soldiers **slaughter** livestock.
retaliate (ch. 8)	take revenge	People who are angry about their losses sometimes try to **retaliate**.
sedition (ch. 8)	treason; rebellion	It is hard for Tim to realize that Sam supports **sedition** by fighting for the Patriots.
headstrong (ch. 8)	reckless; willful	Father thinks that Sam is **headstrong**, and Tim thinks he's daring.
wharf (ch. 8)	pier or dock	Fishing boats tie up at the **wharf** each night.
Johnny cake (ch. 8)	cornmeal cake	**Johnny cake** is delicious with hot gravy.
unconscious (ch. 9)	lifeless; not aware	Tim worries that Father is injured or lying **unconscious** somewhere.

Name _____

Date _____

Understanding Vocabulary Words

Directions: The following words appear in this section of the book. Use context clues and reference materials to determine an accurate definition for each word.

Word	Definition
enlistment (ch. 7)	
recalcitrance (ch. 7)	
grimace (ch. 7)	
slaughter (ch. 8)	
retaliate (ch. 8)	
sedition (ch. 8)	
headstrong (ch. 8)	
wharf (ch. 8)	
Johnny cake (ch. 8)	
unconscious (ch. 9)	

Name _____

Date _____

During-Reading Vocabulary Activity

Directions: As you read these chapters, record at least eight important words on the lines below. Try to find interesting, difficult, intriguing, special, or funny words. Your words can be long or short. They can be hard or easy to spell. After each word, use context clues in the text and reference materials to define the word.

- _____
- _____
- _____
- _____
- _____
- _____
- _____
- _____
- _____
- _____

Directions: Now, organize your words. Rewrite each of your words on a sticky note. Work as a group to create a bar graph of your words. You should stack any words that are the same on top of one another. Different words appear in different columns. Finally, discuss with your teacher why certain words were chosen more often than other words.

Analyzing the Literature

Provided below are discussion questions you can use in small groups, with the whole class, or for written assignments. Each question is given at two levels so you can choose the right question for each group of students. Activity sheets with these questions are provided (pages 38–39) if you want students to write their responses. For each question, a few key discussion points are provided for your reference.

Story Element	■ Level 1	▲ Level 2	Key Discussion Points
Plot	Why does Father go to Verplancks Point each year?	Describe what Father takes into consideration while he plans for the trip to Verplancks Point.	Father goes to Verplancks Point to sell their beef. They wait as late in the fall as possible, trying to go just before the snows begin. The prices for beef increase as meat becomes scarce.
Character	How does Father react to being stopped by the cow-boys?	Contrast Father's and Tim's reactions to the cow-boys. Do you think Father is hiding his feelings? Why or why not?	Father talks calmly with the cow-boys, as if he's just doing his job. He tells Tim to follow their orders. Tim feels scared and wonders if his dad feels scared.
Setting	What does Tim think about the Hudson River?	How do Father and Tim's reactions to the Hudson River differ?	Tim finds the river to be beautiful. The hills are craggy and rocky. It also looks like it would be fun to live there—more fun than being a tavern keeper. There are boats and people fishing. Father explains that fishing is hard work.
Plot	How does Tim outsmart the cow-boys at the end of chapter 9?	What do you think is happening to Father?	Tim pretends that there is an escort coming for him. This saves their supplies. Possible answers regarding Father include being injured, trying to get help, being captured by soldiers, and so forth.

Name _____

Date _____

Analyzing the Literature

Directions: Think about the section you just read. Read each question and state your response with textual evidence.

1. Why does Father go to Verplancks Point each year?

_____

_____

_____

_____

2. How does Father react to being stopped by the cow-boys?

_____

_____

_____

_____

3. What does Tim think about the Hudson River?

_____

_____

_____

_____

4. How does Tim outsmart the cow-boys at the end of chapter 9?

_____

_____

_____

_____

Name _____

Date _____

▲ Analyzing the Literature

Directions: Think about the section you just read. Read each question and state your response with textual evidence.

1. Describe what Father takes into consideration while he plans for the trip to Verplancks Point.

_____

_____

_____

_____

2. Contrast Father's and Tim's reactions to the cow-boys. Do you think Father is hiding his feelings? Why or why not?

_____

_____

_____

_____

3. How do Father and Tim's reactions to the Hudson River differ?

_____

_____

_____

_____

4. What do you think is happening to Father?

_____

_____

_____

Name _____

Date _____

Reader Response

Directions: Choose one of the following prompts about this section to answer. Be sure you include a topic sentence in your response, use textual evidence to support your opinion, and provide a strong conclusion that summarizes your opinion.

Writing Prompts

- **Narrative Piece**—Tim discovers the wonders of travel when he sees the Hudson River. Compare his reaction to a time when you've gone someplace new and fascinating.
- **Informative/Explanatory Piece**—In this section, Tim faces difficult challenges. Explain how he has grown up. For example, you could contrast how he handles himself with the cow-boys to his earlier effort to get a message to Mr. Heron.

_____

_____

_____

_____

_____

_____

_____

_____

_____

_____

_____

_____

_____

Close Reading the Literature

Directions: Closely reread the last eight paragraphs in chapter 7, beginning with, "This time they didn't even turn around to look at me." Read to the end of the chapter. Read each question, then revisit the text to find the evidence that supports your answer.

1. Refer to the first paragraph in the section to explain Tim's plan for getting help.

   _____

   _____

   _____

2. Describe Father's injuries, using evidence from the text in your description.

   _____

   _____

   _____

3. How does Father avoid saying that he is a Loyalist?

   _____

   _____

   _____

4. According to the text, how does Tim feel about stepping across the line into New York?

   _____

   _____

   _____

   _____

Name _____

Date _____

Making Connections–Missing in Action

Directions: Although Father is not a soldier, he is indeed missing. Create a "missing" poster that gives information about Father. Include details about his appearance, with reference to his injuries. The poster should state where he disappears with a sketch of the area. Include contact information for his family.

Name _____

Date _____

Creating with the Story Elements

Directions: Thinking about the story elements of character, setting, and plot in a novel is very important to understanding what is happening and why. Complete **one** of the following activities about what you've read so far. Be creative and have fun!

Characters

Think about words that describe Sam. For example his father calls him *headstrong*. Find three descriptive words for Sam from each point of view: Father, Mother, Tim, and Betsy. Recreate this chart with your descriptive words.

All About Sam

	Three Descriptive Words
Father	
Mother	
Tim	
Betsy	

Setting

Verplancks Point was purchased from the American Indians on August 24, 1683, for wampum, rum, beer, knives, and trinkets. Although no longer on most maps, it was located about eight miles north of Ossining, New York. Recreate the route that Tim and Father walk from Redding to just north of Ossining, New York. Label the map with towns and cities that exist today. Use the map showing the route at the beginning of the book for your comparison.

Plot

The ending to chapter 9 is a "cliffhanger"—we don't know where Father is. Make a drawing of a climb up a slope to a cliff. Label at least five events from the story that lead up to this point. They should be key plot points. The drawing and events should summarize the story. The last event should be the capture of Father.

Vocabulary Overview

Ten key words from this section are provided below with definitions and sentences about how the words are used in the book. Choose one of the vocabulary activity sheets (pages 45 or 46) for students to complete as they read this section. Monitor students as they work to ensure the definitions they have found are accurate and relate to the text. Finally, discuss these important vocabulary words with students. If you think these words or other words in the section warrant more time devoted to them, there are suggestions in the introduction for other vocabulary activities (page 5).

Word	Definition	Sentence about Text
depreciation (ch. 10)	decline; lessen	The war causes a **depreciation** in the value of paper money.
commotion (ch. 10)	uproar	Just after making a **commotion**, the soldiers shoot a rebel.
fusillade (ch. 10)	series of shots	A man is shot and wounded during the **fusillade**.
munitions (ch. 11)	weapons	The wounded man tells Tim that the soldiers are after the Rebels' **munitions**.
desertion (ch. 11)	running away	**Desertion** from the army is cause for hanging.
badgered (ch. 11)	pestered; nagged	Sam complains that Tim **badgered** him about coming home.
epidemic (ch. 12)	outbreak	Many people can die from an **epidemic** of cholera in prison.
siege (ch. 12)	barricade; blocking supplies	People can't get food from White Plains because the Rebels have the town under **siege**.
unscrupulous (ch. 12)	dishonest	People who are hungry may become **unscrupulous** and steal food.
forage (ch. 12)	hunt; search	People will be upset if the troops **forage** for food on their farms.

Name _____

Date _____

Understanding Vocabulary Words

Directions: The following words appear in this section of the book. Use context clues and reference materials to determine an accurate definition for each word.

Word	Definition
depreciation (ch. 10)	
commotion (ch. 10)	
fusillade (ch. 10)	
munitions (ch. 11)	
desertion (ch. 11)	
badgered (ch. 11)	
epidemic (ch. 12)	
siege (ch. 12)	
unscrupulous (ch. 12)	
forage (ch. 12)	

Name _____

Date _____

During-Reading Vocabulary Activity

Directions: As you read these chapters, record at least eight important words on the lines below. Try to find interesting, difficult, intriguing, special, or funny words. Your words can be long or short. They can be hard or easy to spell. After each word, use context clues in the text and reference materials to define the word.

- _____
- _____
- _____
- _____
- _____
- _____
- _____
- _____
- _____

Directions: Respond to these questions about the words in this section.

1. Why do some people, including Mother, think the British soldiers are **brutes**?

   _____

   _____

2. In chapter 12, what does Tim mean when he says that he has to **tread water** until the war is over?

   _____

   _____

   _____

Analyzing the Literature

Provided below are discussion questions you can use in small groups, with the whole class, or for written assignments. Each question is given at two levels so you can choose the right question for each group of students. Activity sheets with these questions are provided (pages 48–49) if you want students to write their responses. For each question, a few key discussion points are provided for your reference.

Story Element	■ Level 1	▲ Level 2	Key Discussion Points
Setting	What is it like when the British arrive in the village?	When the British arrive, Tim wonders how the Rebels could win. What does he see that makes him doubt the Rebels?	Hundreds, possibly thousands of British soldiers arrive with cannons, wagons, supplies, and horses. They wear impressive uniforms and seem well trained.
Plot	Why are people so hungry?	How does Tim describe hunger in chapter 12?	Most of the animals have been killed and eaten. Tim compares hunger to having a nail in your shoe. You can't forget about it. You feel weak, and you get sick more easily.
Character	What does Mr. Heron do after the British arrive?	Do you think Mr. Heron was right to tell the British where Rebel sympathizers lived? Why or why not?	Mr. Heron informs on other village residents, and several villagers are killed, including the boy Jerry Sanford. It's not clear what Mr. Heron's motivations are. Discuss the challenges with taking sides, turning on neighbors, and so forth.
Plot	What happens to Father? Do you think that is fair? Why or why not?	Why does Tim say it is "funny" that his father died on a *British* prison ship?	Discuss how Father is loyal to the British; yet, they won't believe him, evidently. He might have survived imprisonment with better conditions. Epidemics, such as those from cholera, generally ignore political preferences, striking anyone in a weakened condition.

Name _____

Date _____

Analyzing the Literature

Directions: Think about the section you just read. Read each question and state your response with textual evidence.

1. What is it like when the British arrive in the village?

_____

_____

_____

_____

2. Why are people so hungry?

_____

_____

_____

_____

3. What does Mr. Heron do after the British arrive?

_____

_____

_____

_____

4. What happens to Father? Do you think that is fair? Why or why not?

_____

_____

_____

_____

Name _____

Date _____

▲ Analyzing the Literature

Directions: Think about the section you just read. Read each question and state your response with textual evidence.

1. When the British arrive, Tim wonders how the Rebels could win. What does he see that makes him doubt the Rebels?

   _____

   _____

   _____

   _____

2. How does Tim describe hunger in chapter 12?

   _____

   _____

   _____

   _____

3. Do you think Mr. Heron was right to tell the British where Rebel sympathizers lived? Why or why not?

   _____

   _____

   _____

   _____

4. Why does Tim say it is "funny" that his father died on a *British* prison ship?

   _____

   _____

   _____

Name _____

Date _____

Reader Response

Directions: Choose one of the following prompts about this section to answer. Be sure you include a topic sentence in your response, use textual evidence to support your opinion, and provide a strong conclusion that summarizes your opinion.

Writing Prompts

- **Informative/Explanatory Piece**—Mother refuses to let Tim take more risks. She says she's lost enough. Describe how your mother would react if faced with the same circumstances. Explain why she would—or wouldn't—let you get further involved.
- **Opinion/Argument Piece**—People often say that war isn't fair. Think about the unfair events that have happened so far in the story. Write about the event that you believe is most unfair. Support your opinion with details.

_____

_____

_____

_____

_____

_____

_____

_____

_____

_____

_____

_____

Name _____

Date _____

Close Reading the Literature

Directions: Closely reread the section in the middle of chapter 10 that begins with, "So there were a lot of changes . . . ." Read five paragraphs. Read each question, then revisit the text to find the evidence that supports your answer.

1. Describe Tim's memory of how he used to act at breakfast *before* his trip to Verplancks Point.

   _____

   _____

   _____

2. Use Tim's behavior at breakfast *after* his trip to Verplancks Point to describe how he's changed.

   _____

   _____

   _____

3. Do you think Tim is more of a child or an adult since going to Verplancks Point? Justify your choice based on Tim's thinking in this section.

   _____

   _____

   _____

4. Explain why Tim is angry at Sam. Find evidence to support your reason.

   _____

   _____

   _____

   _____

Name _____

Date _____

Making Connections—Dinner Time!

The soldiers are supposed to get a variety of food. However, they live mostly on bread and meat. They rarely get vegetables. Soldiers have to prepare their own meals. The following is a typical ration for one day:

Daily Ration

- 1 pound of beef or $\frac{1}{2}$ pound of salt pork
- 1 pound of flour for making bread
- 1 pint of peas or cornmeal
- salt
- 1 gallon of water or other beverage

Directions: You are now in charge of rations. Plan how much you need for 100 and 1,000 soldiers for one day. Then, answer the questions below.

	Total for 100 soldiers	Total for 1,000 soldiers
beef		
salt pork		
flour		
peas/ cornmeal		
water		

1. What foods would you add to the list if you had the budget? Remember, the soldiers have to cook their own food.

   _____

   _____

2. What challenges would you face in providing for the soldiers during winter?

   _____

   _____

Name _____

Date _____

Creating with the Story Elements

Directions: Thinking about the story elements of character, setting, and plot in a novel is very important to understanding what is happening and why. Complete **one** of the following activities about what you've read so far. Be creative and have fun!

Characters

The trip to Verplancks Point is a turning point in Tim's life. Draw a line down the center of a piece of paper. Write *Before Verplancks Point* on the left side and *After Verplancks Point* on the right side. Write a paragraph about Tim's characteristics in each section.

Setting

Recreate the scene near the end of chapter 10. Tim is watching the troops and listening to the shooting. Create a drawing or diorama that depicts the soldiers, the killings, and the general chaos. Think about the five senses for your creation: sight, smell, taste, touch, and hearing.

Plot

You know from the title of the novel that Sam must die at some point in this book. Think about the key events in the story. Choose three events. Create a story map for each event showing the possible reasons for Sam's death.

Vocabulary Overview

Ten key words from this section are provided below with definitions and sentences about how the words are used in the book. Choose one of the vocabulary activity sheets (pages 55 or 56) for students to complete as they read this section. Monitor students as they work to ensure the definitions they have found are accurate and relate to the text. Finally, discuss these important vocabulary words with students. If you think these words or other words in the section warrant more time devoted to them, there are suggestions in the introduction for other vocabulary activities (page 5).

Word	Definition	Sentence about Text
adjutant (ch. 13)	assistant; aide	Tim speaks to the **adjutant**, Colonel Parsons's assistant.
encampment (ch. 13)	army camp	Sam is taken to the **encampment**.
foreboding (ch. 13)	bad feeling	Mother has a **foreboding** that something bad is going to happen.
officially (ch. 13)	formally	**Officially**, according to the rules, Sam was not at his post.
execute (ch. 13)	kill	They would **execute** the butcher by hanging him.
destruction (ch. 13)	damage	War causes great **destruction**, ruining property and lives.
clemency (ch. 13)	mercy; kindness	It would be a kindness if the general could show **clemency** and not execute Sam.
gallows (ch. 14)	scaffold or structure for hanging or execution	The **gallows** stand on a hill, ready for the hangings.
muzzles (ch. 14)	ends of guns	The bullets come out of the **muzzles** of guns.
prospered (epilogue)	flourished; succeeded	He **prospered** over the years, doing well in life.

Name _____

Date _____

Understanding Vocabulary Words

Directions: The following words appear in this section of the book. Use context clues and reference materials to determine an accurate definition for each word.

Word	Definition
adjutant (ch. 13)	
encampment (ch. 13)	
foreboding (ch. 13)	
officially (ch. 13)	
execute (ch. 13)	
destruction (ch. 13)	
clemency (ch. 13)	
gallows (ch. 14)	
muzzles (ch. 14)	
prospered (epilogue)	

Name _____

Date _____

During-Reading Vocabulary Activity

Directions: As you read these chapters, choose five important words from the story. Use these words to complete the word flow chart below. On each arrow, write a word. In each box, explain how the connected pair of words relates to each other. An example for the words *foreboding* and *clemency* has been done for you.

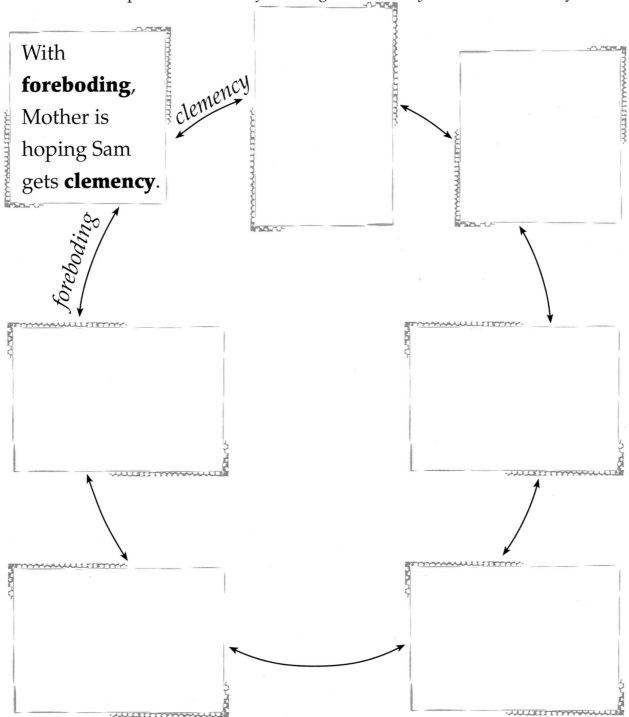

With **foreboding**, Mother is hoping Sam gets **clemency**.

Analyzing the Literature

Provided below are discussion questions you can use in small groups, with the whole class, or for written assignments. Each question is given at two levels so you can choose the right question for each group of students. Activity sheets with these questions are provided (pages 58–59) if you want students to write their responses. For each question, a few key discussion points are provided for your reference.

Story Element	■ Level 1	▲ Level 2	Key Discussion Points
Character	How does Mother react to Sam's sentence?	Do you think Mother is justified in giving up? How would your mother react to losing her husband and one child?	Discuss how Mother is worn down from the war, plus the many losses. She feels helpless and unable to change anything. If time allows, compare the frustration from a male and female point of view.
Character	How does Tim try to save Sam? Is he wise or foolish?	What does Tim's effort to save Sam tell you about him? Would you have done the same? Why or why not?	Tim tries to throw a musket into the stockade. He is desperate to help his brother. Some students may feel that he is brave. Some may think he is foolish.
Setting	Tim races away from the stockade after he throws the musket. What is the area like that he runs through?	How does the surrounding area help Tim get away after he throws the musket into the stockade? What might have happened to him in an open field?	Discuss how the area has boulders, trees, a hill, and snow fields for hiding. In an open field he might be easier to shoot.
Plot	Is it right to make an example of Sam? Why or why not?	Describe the decision to execute Sam from the general's point of view. Is it justified for the "greater good"?	Discuss how in times of war leaders must make tough decisions. Sometimes, the truth is not easy to determine, making leadership especially difficult. Leaders are sometimes wrong, believing people who have lied to save themselves.

Name _____

Date _____

Analyzing the Literature

Directions: Think about the section you just read. Read each question and state your response with textual evidence.

1. How does Mother react to Sam's sentence?

   _____

   _____

   _____

   _____

2. How does Tim try to save Sam? Is he wise or foolish?

   _____

   _____

   _____

   _____

3. Tim races away from the stockade after he throws the musket. What is the area like that he runs through?

   _____

   _____

   _____

   _____

4. Is it right to make an example of Sam? Why or why not?

   _____

   _____

   _____

   _____

Name _____

Date _____

▲ Analyzing the Literature

Directions: Think about the section you just read. Read each question and state your response with textual evidence.

1. Do you think Mother is justified in giving up? How would your mother react to losing her husband and one child?

   _____

   _____

   _____

2. What does Tim's effort to save Sam tell you about him? Would you have done the same? Why or why not?

   _____

   _____

   _____

3. How does the surrounding area help Tim get away after he throws the musket into the stockade? What might have happened to him in an open field?

   _____

   _____

   _____

   _____

4. Describe the decision to execute Sam from the general's point of view. Is it justified for the "greater good"?

   _____

   _____

   _____

   _____

Name _____

Date _____

Reader Response

Directions: Choose one of the following prompts about this section to answer. Be sure you include a topic sentence in your response, use textual evidence to support your opinion, and provide a strong conclusion that summarizes your opinion.

Writing Prompts

- **Narrative Piece**—Think about how people now use social media to cause change. What could Tim do in today's world to influence Colonel Parsons? Write a convincing argument to free Sam as a blog, series of tweets, or a letter to the editor of an online magazine.
- **Informative/Explanatory Piece**—Think about the differences between how Tim and his mother live after the war. Contrast their choices and explain why they differ so much.

_____

_____

_____

_____

_____

_____

_____

_____

_____

_____

_____

_____

Name _____

Date _____

Close Reading the Literature

Directions: Closely reread the epilogue. Read each question, then revisit the text to find the evidence that supports your answer.

1. Using the details in this section, describe what Tim is like in 1826.

   _____

   _____

   _____

2. For what reasons don't Tim and Mother move away right after Sam's death?

   _____

   _____

   _____

3. What text evidence helps the reader understand how Tim benefits from learning surveying?

   _____

   _____

   _____

   _____

4. How does Mother adjust after Sam's death? What are examples of her life from after the war?

   _____

   _____

   _____

   _____

Name _____

Date _____

Making Connections–Selling the Movie

Directions: Design a poster that advertises a movie of *My Brother Sam Is Dead*. Think about movie posters you've seen or look at some online. Include things such as the title, a short summary, and some descriptive words. Other things to consider include people you'd want to star in the movie, a director, opening details, and so forth. Make people *want* to see the movie!

Name _____

Date _____

Creating with the Story Elements

Directions: Thinking about the story elements of character, setting, and plot in a novel is very important to understanding what is happening and why. Complete **one** of the following activities about what you've read so far. Be creative and have fun!

Characters

Find a partner and flip a coin to decide who will be King George and who will be George Washington. Create a mock debate with King George reflecting the point of view of Father's character. George Washington should respond from Sam's point of view. Present your debate to a third character who, like Tim, is undecided. Who makes the most telling points?

Setting

Create a map of the encampment. Reference the map at the beginning of the book, enlarging the encampment section to include the following: gallows, stockade, boulders, trees, and so forth. Indicate where Tim is hit as he escapes.

Plot

Choose one event from this section and compare it to a current or recent event. For example, you might compare Sam's court-martial to a recent or current trial. Create a compare and contrast chart showing how the events are alike and different.

Name _____

Date _____

Post-Reading Theme Thoughts

Directions: Read each of the statements in the first column. Choose a main character from *My Brother Sam Is Dead*. Think about that character's point of view. From that character's perspective, decide if the character would agree or disagree with the statements. Record the character's opinion by marking an *X* in Agree or Disagree for each statement. Explain your choices in the fourth column using text evidence.

Character I Chose: _____

Statement	Agree	Disagree	Explain Your Answer
It's okay to steal food to survive.			
Families should stick together during tough times.			
A teenager can rebel if he or she thinks a parent is wrong.			
Killing during times of war is always justified.			

Name _____

Date _____

Culminating Activity: Time Capsule

Directions: Once Sam is in the stockade, he knows that he will probably die. Create a list of at least 10 things that Sam might want to place in a time capsule. Think about key events in the book, such as when he steals the musket, his letters to Betsy, and so forth. Consider items that are not in the story, but that reflect the war in general.

- _____

- _____

- _____

- _____

- _____

- _____

- _____

- _____

- _____

- _____

Name _____

Date _____

Culminating Activity:
Time Capsule (cont.)

Directions: Choose three different times in history for when the time capsule could be opened. Think about significant events in history, such as anniversaries of the war, when future generations might appreciate it, or when Tim might want it opened. In the organizer below, describe the celebrations that would take place at the openings of the time capsule.

Date for opening	Reason for the chosen date	Celebratory activities for the opening	People to invite

Name _____

Date _____

Comprehension Assessment

Directions: Circle the best response to each question.

1. What is the meaning of British **domination** as it is used in this novel?

     A. the Rebels' fight against the British

     B. the control over Father on the British prison ship

     C. the Loyalists' belief in the right of the king

     D. the control the British have over the colonies

2. Which detail from the book best supports your answer to question 1?

     E. Tim's decision to write a book to commemorate Sam.

     F. Tim's description of how the nation prospers after beating the British.

     G. Mother's refusal to serve officers of the Continental Army.

     H. Loyalists like Father believe that the king should rule over the colonies.

3. What is the main idea of this text? (Right before this quotation, Tim has told his mother that he's going to save Sam.)

     "No, you're not," she said in a soft whispery kind of a voice. "No, you're going to get yourself killed. Well you might as well. Let's have it all done with at once. How does the old line go? Men must fight and women must weep, but you'll get no more tears from me. I've done my weeping for this war."

     _____

     _____

     _____

     _____

     _____

4. Which **two** details support your answer to question 3?

     A. Sam is sure that he can do something for his brother.

     B. Men used to go off to fight in wars, leaving women behind.

     C. Mother refuses to go to church.

     D. Mother knows that nothing can be done to help Sam.

Comprehension Assessment (cont.)

5. Which statement best expresses one of the themes of the novel?

    E. Leaders are always right and should be respected.

    F. Friends never take different sides.

    G. Life is not always fair, especially during wartime.

    H. Only the dead find peace during war.

6. Which detail from the novel provides the best evidence for your answer to number 5?

    A. "I've just seen General Putnam. He said he'd consider your case."

    B. "We closed the tavern early that night. Nobody was there, anyway."

    C. "The other men lied . . . . They had a story all worked out."

    D. "I'm going to save my brother."

7. Explain the purpose of this sentence from the novel: *Father said, "In war the dead pay the debts of the living."*

    _____

    _____

    _____

    _____

    _____

8. Which other quotation from the story serves a similar purpose.

    E. "Perhaps . . . somebody will read this and see what the cost has been."

    F. "His war record is good and that'll help."

    G. "I thought he was a man of greater patriotism . . . ."

    H. "What does the life of one more man mean to them?"

Name _____

Date _____

Response to Literature: Effects of War

Directions: Think about the impact the Revolutionary War had on the Meeker family's way of life. Summarize the impacts in the chart.

Way of Life	Impact
food	
work or livelihood	
friendships	
politics	
religion	
future	

Directions: Assume that the Revolutionary War has not yet started. Write a letter to King George III explaining why he should grant the colonies their independence *without* resorting to war. Use the effects of war (summarized above) to make a compelling argument to support your opinion. Be persuasive.

_____

_____

_____

_____

_____

_____

Name _____

Date _____

Response to Literature Rubric

Directions: Use this rubric to evaluate student responses.

	Exceptional Writing	Quality Writing	Developing Writing
Focus and Organization	☐ States a clear opinion and elaborates well. Engages the reader from hook through the middle to the conclusion. Demonstrates clear understanding of the intended audience and purpose of the piece.	☐ Provides a clear and consistent opinion. Maintains a clear perspective and supports it through elaborating details. Makes the opinion clear in the opening hook and summarizes well in the conclusion.	☐ Provides an inconsistent point of view. Does not support the topic adequately or misses pertinent information. Provides lack of clarity in the beginning, middle, and conclusion.
Text Evidence	☐ Provides comprehensive and accurate support. Includes relevant and worthwhile text references.	☐ Provides limited support. Provides few supporting text references.	☐ Provides very limited support for the text. Provides no supporting text references.
Written Expression	☐ Uses descriptive and precise language with clarity and intention. Maintains a consistent voice and uses an appropriate tone that supports meaning. Uses multiple sentence types and transitions well between ideas.	☐ Uses a broad vocabulary. Maintains a consistent voice and supports a tone and feelings through language. Varies sentence length and word choices.	☐ Uses a limited and unvaried vocabulary. Provides an inconsistent or weak voice and tone. Provides little to no variation in sentence type and length.
Language Conventions	☐ Capitalizes, punctuates, and spells accurately. Demonstrates complete thoughts within sentences, with accurate subject-verb agreement. Uses paragraphs appropriately and with clear purpose.	☐ Capitalizes, punctuates, and spells accurately. Demonstrates complete thoughts within sentences and appropriate grammar. Paragraphs are properly divided and supported.	☐ Incorrectly capitalizes, punctuates, and spells. Uses fragmented or run-on sentences. Utilizes poor grammar overall. Paragraphs are poorly divided and developed.

© Shell Education

The responses provided here are just examples of what students may answer. Many accurate responses are possible for the questions throughout this unit.

During-Reading Vocabulary Activity—Section 1: Chapters 1–3 (page 16)

1. Father refuses to have anything said in his house that might be considered **treason**, or disloyal to the king.

2. Sam must be smart because he scores telling points in debates. He also knows pretty girls, which might be considered a **triumph**.

Close Reading the Literature—Section 1: Chapters 1–3 (page 21)

1. Examples include: a man with his throat cut, begging for grace and a man shrieks when he feels a bayonet go through him. A secondary response might be the sounds of celebration during the bonfires.

2. Father does not want him coming home in a sack or in a wagon, dead.

3. Sam refuses to take off his uniform. He tells Father that he can't order him around and that he's a man.

4. Father is crying and telling Tim that things will be bad.

Making Connections—Section 1: Chapters 1–3 (page 22)

These are possible answers for the **Father's Reaction** column:

- Father reacts with tears at Sam's decision to join the army.
- Father believes that Sam should not argue with his parents.
- Father is upset and worried when Sam takes the gun.

During-Reading Vocabulary Activity—Section 2: Chapters 4–6 (page 26)

1. The Patriots are **underdogs** because they are not as well equipped to fight, without new uniforms or weapons.

2. Tim thinks he is being **dishonorable** because he plans to disobey his father and deliver the letter.

Close Reading the Literature—Section 2: Chapters 4–6 (page 31)

1. War stories include: hearing about someone being killed, finding fresh bodies in a field, meeting someone wounded, and knowing people who have been in a battle.

2. The war seems far away. The events don't feel like they could happen to Tim.

3. He says that the search for weapons makes him realize that war could affect him directly. His father has been punched.

4. People use guns for hunting, for killing wolves, and for general protection.

Close Reading the Literature—Section 3: Chapters 7–9 (page 41)

1. Tim begins to run across the fields to find a farmhouse and people who can help.

2. Father has a cut on his head that is bleeding and a smaller cut over his eye. He also has a black and blue eye.

3. Father says that he is interested in making a living, not fighting a war.

4. Tim expected that it would be different, referring to this other colony, New York, as a foreign country. Instead, he finds it is just like being at home.

During-Reading Vocabulary Activity—Section 4: Chapters 10–12 (page 46)

1. Some people think the British soldiers are **brutes** because they are taking food and land. They are abusive to possible Patriots.

2. Tim knows that he has to keep working no matter what or his family's tavern might sink, which means he has to **tread water**.

Close Reading the Literature—Section 4: Chapters 10–12 (page 51)

1. Before the trip to Verplancks Point, Tim usually took his time at breakfast. He ate slowly, stalling before getting to work.

2. After the trip, Tim immediately begins planning his work, without stalling.

3. Answers will vary, but Tim thinks he is more of an adult, though not totally grown up.

4. Tim is angry because Sam fights for the Rebels, leaving Tim to do all the work.

Making Connections—Section 4: Chapters 10–12 (page 52)

	Total for 100 soldiers	Total for 1,000 soldiers
beef	100 pounds	1,000 pounds
salt pork	50 pounds	500 pounds
flour	100 pounds	1,000 pounds
peas/cornmeal	100 pints	1,000 pints
water	100 gallons	1,000 gallons

1. Answers will vary.

2. Answers may include the weather, lack of food, lack of money, and so forth.

Close Reading the Literature—Section 5: Chapters 13–Epilogue (page 61)

1. Tim is 64, in good health, and he's had a happy life. He's been successful.

2. The war goes on for three more years. It is hard for Tim or Mother to think about building a new life.

3. Tim states that he bought and sold land, which uses surveying skills.

4. Mother refuses to serve Continental officers. However, she does tell stories about Sam as she ages, and she enjoys her grandchildren and new life.

Comprehension Assessment (pages 67–68)

1. D. the control the British have over the colonies

2. H. Loyalists like Father believe that the king should rule over the colonies.

3. Main idea: Mother has given up; she's letting Sam go.

4. B. Men used to go off to fight in wars, leaving women behind. D. Mother knows that nothing can be done to help Sam.

5. G. Life is not always fair, especially during wartime.

6. C. "The other men lied . . . . They had a story all worked out."

7. That people who die give up their lives for others, for those who survive.

8. E. "Perhaps . . . somebody will read this and see what the cost has been."